Foundations of Dreams and Journeys

On the road with mismatched pairs,
One's too tight, the other's in the airs.
Prancing like a clown in a fancy dress,
Every step feels like a comic mess.

Kick them off when the sun is high,
Grab a ride on a friendly fly.
With rubber bands and socks that squeak,
We're off to find the next great peak.

The blisters dance on my left foot,
While my right one's got a shiny boot.
Who needs style when the path is funny?
Laughter's sweet, not just for money!

So trudge along with happy feet,
Through puddles, mud, and tasty treats.
Each leap and slide brings joy anew,
Foundations built on the silly view!

The Map Crafted in My Soles

In a pair of old sneakers, I found my way,
They squeak like a duck, come what may.
With every step, the ground bids me dance,
And strangers just laugh at my clumsy prance.

A flip-flop on one foot, a boot on the other,
My wardrobe's a joke, oh dear, what a bother!
Each footprint a map, leading me astray,
But I skip through the chaos, and live for today.

Balancing Dreams on the Ground

Worn-out sandals, ready for play,
They wobble and tilt, oh please stay at bay.
I juggle my dreams, while tripping on grass,
Who knew that my path could be such a farce?

My left foot believes it found the right place,
While my right foot's certain it's lost in space.
Together they laugh, like a duo quite bold,
Making each step an adventure retold.

Each Step a New Horizon

Each step I take feels like a twist,
My laces collide in a tangled list.
I leap like a frog, and roll like a ball,
With each little hop, I feel ten feet tall.

The pavement laughs back, as I dance on the spot,
With shoes way too big, but hey, why not?
Around every corner, a giggle, a cheer,
It's a comical journey, let's give a big leer!

Soul and Sole: Connected Journeys

My left sole is snoring, my right one awake,
Together they argue, for goodness' sake!
With each step we take, it's a wobbly race,
A toe on a mission, a heel full of grace.

The adventures we seek leave us grinning like fools,
Through puddles and mud, breaking all of the rules.
We stumble, we giggle, it's all part of the show,
These soles on this mission, just go with the flow!

Walking Between Worlds

With every step, a sock may peek,
A mismatched pair, oh what a cheek!
I wander off, a dreamer's plight,
In sandals bright, not quite polite.

A bow and lace, they make a deal,
To dance upon my toes, surreal.
Each clumsy step, an artful trip,
Halfway to space on rubber grip.

A puddle waits, my fate it schemes,
Splashing laughter, rending seams.
Whimsy leads, the ground I greet,
With socks that smell like last week's feet.

In worlds of mud, I spin and hop,
Where grass is green and never stops.
I leap from here, I dash from there,
In this fine dance of shoeless air.

The Fabric of Footprints

A tattered sole, a tale untold,
Of journeys past, both brave and bold.
With every mark upon the earth,
Lies laughter, dreams, and silly mirth.

From cookie crumbs to mountain trails,
I've left my prints where whimsy sails.
A footprint here, a splash of foam,
Every step a giggle, a roam.

In flip-flops loud or boots of pride,
I conquer mud, the world my slide.
The fabric of my path's delight,
Woven in joy from day to night.

On rainy days when skies are gray,
Do dance with me upon the way.
Each footprint's stitched with laughter loud,
A quilt of joy, my laughter shroud.

Grounded in Exploration

Each toe a compass, wiggling free,
Pointing to all the fun to be.
A stony road or grassy glide,
With every step, I take on pride.

The world unfolds like magic maps,
With friendly bees and giggly chaps.
I trudge through leaves, a crunchy sound,
Lost in the joy that I have found.

A treasure hunt for lost old shoes,
In fields of grass, I chase the blues.
With every trip and every twist,
There's laughter waiting, can't resist!

Through puddles deep and deserts dry,
Adventures call, they never lie.
I stumble, tumble, laugh and grin,
For life's a dance, let's spin again!

Odyssey of the Sole

I've wandered far on mismatched pair,
With one heel high and one in air.
An epic quest on wobbly feet,
Each pebble felt, each slip a treat.

Through sticky gum and chewing woes,
My soles are stung by thorny rows.
Yet every ouch becomes a laugh,
In this grand saga, I'm the half.

The path is lined with quirky finds,
Old sneakers peeking, all sorts of kinds.
A cardboard map and compass missing,
But oh, it's joy that's truly kissing!

So join the fun, don't mind the trip,
Let's race the wind, a joyous skip.
As long as feet can feel the ground,
This odyssey's where fun is found.

Tracks of the Free Spirit

In bright red sneakers, I float through the park,
Feet with a purpose, not a whim or a lark.
A great leap ahead, on a path lined with cheer,
But wait—my shoe's untied, oh dear, oh dear!

With flip-flops and sandals, my style's quite bold,
Yet every step squeaks, like a story retold.
I waddle and wobble, my laughter a sound,
As I kick off my shoes, and dance all around!

The Rapture of the Journey

In loafers too tight, I shuffle and skate,
Each step is a gamble, and oh, isn't fate great?
Walking like a penguin for all to behold,
It's harder than it seems, or so I am told.

With bright neon laces, my feet spring to life,
I twirl and I trip—oh, what a fun strife!
The ground feels like quicksand as I traverse,
But laughter is gold, and this folly's diverse!

Steps of Serenity

In ballet flats bouncing through puddles of glee,
Each splash is a giggle, so silly and free.
I dance on the pavement, my style's all askew,
With wiggling toes, I shout, 'Look at me too!'

With boots that are clunky, I stomp on the ground,
Every step I conquer creates joyful sound.
Each stride tells a tale, a riddle, a jest,
In a world of odd steps, I know I'm the best!

Journey through Fabric and Leather

With my sandals adorned, I swagger with flair,
The summer sun shines, and I'm caught in the air!
But oh! Are those snares? A rogue piece of gum,
I pluck and I dance, 'cause I'm never so glum!

In stilettos, I twirl, what a wobbly sight,
Like a flamingo chasing a butterfly's flight.
Strutting like a queen on a stage made of dreams,
Life's hall of mishaps is bursting with gleams!

Strapping on Hope

With laces tied and ready to go,
I stumble and trip, oh what a show!
These clunky boots, they squeak and squeal,
Like a comedic act, that's just too real.

Each step I take, my socks do slide,
It's a dance of chaos, oh what a ride!
But laughter bursts, even in the fall,
Making memories the best of all.

Steps of Silent Stories

Each pair of sneakers tells a tale,
From muddy paths to a slippery trail.
They squeak and pitter-patter in glee,
As if they whisper secrets to me.

A flip-flop flop, a clumsy stumble,
Oh, the laughter, oh how I tumble!
With every step, a giggle ensues,
As my soles get lost in the mischief of shoes.

The Call of the Unseen Trail

I lace them up for the unknown spree,
But they have plans, oh woe is me!
One shoe's loose, the other's tight,
Like a pair in a comedic fight.

I wander off with a chuckle and grin,
As my left foot decides it won't begin.
The sidewalk calls, but I just might fall,
On this crooked path, I'll be the clown of them all.

Journey with Every Click

With every click, my heels do sing,
As if they know the joy they bring.
They tap dance happily, having their fun,
But watch out, dear friend, the journey's begun!

Through puddles, they splash, oh what a sight,
Causing giggles, oh pure delight.
My feet are the stars of this silly parade,
On this curious trek, memories are made.

Adventures in Every Thread

In a closet full of endless dreams,
Each pair whispers its funny schemes.
One's got a squeak, another's got flair,
But do they care? Not a shoe to spare!

Running late, I grab the bright red pair,
They say 'Zoom!' but I swear they're just rare.
Each step a giggle, each leap a laugh,
Who knew they'd turn me into half a calf?

A stuck zipper here, a heel worn down there,
Yet somehow they all end up fair.
Across puddles and ditching muds,
We're champions at avoiding the thuds!

So when the sun sets, and we've had our fun,
I'll dance to the beat of the shoe's wild run.
With laces untied and stories galore,
Let's twirl in circles—we're never a bore!

Whispers Beneath Us

Underneath my feet, they chatter away,
In colors so bright, they want to play.
Sneakers giggle, while sandals dance,
Every step an awkward romance.

Beneath the chaos of each clumsy stroll,
They hatch plans like they're on a roll.
One's got blisters, the other has flair,
This crazy bunch catches stares everywhere!

Mud gives a wink and rain brings delight,
They stomp and splash, oh what a sight!
I trip and stumble, they just point and grin,
These merry companions—where do I begin?

So next time you scold me for a pratfall,
Remember, it's my soles that are having a ball.
With their whispers and laughter, they embrace the beat,
Together we dance, on this hilarious street!

Chronicles of the Road Taken

On each road I tread, a tale unfolds,
Of mismatched socks and stories bold.
Flip-flops flap, as I jog on by,
While boots stomp down, they seem to sigh.

The sneakers quip, 'Watch us glide!'
While clunky loafers just want to hide.
In shops, they bicker, in parks, they mess,
Like actors in a wild, funny dress!

Late night strolls, the heels they squeak,
A comical tune, a curious streak.
Each pair's a player, on life's grand stage,
Casting laughter, community, and age.

So here's to the stories these soles contrive,
In jumbled paths, we all will thrive.
With every stride, let joy unchain,
In life's absurd journey, we'll dance in the rain!

Beacons Beneath My Feet

They glow and they sparkle, my guiding lights,
Through puddles and laughter, on whimsical nights.
With each little scuff, they narrate their tale,
Of silly encounters and epic derail.

The boots wish for bravery, the flats want some fun,
While slippers just dream of sunbathing done.
Each toe wiggles free, a grand little feast,
As solemates gather, not one is the least!

From trails of green grass to sidewalks of gray,
With every step forward, they freak out and sway.
In worn-out places, they sing with glee,
Together creating a dance of esprit.

So when you feel lost, just look at your feet,
With joyful companions, life's musical beat.
We'll skip and weave, in this world so grand,
With beacons of laughter, hand in hand!

Strides Across the Unknown

With squeaks and creaks, I wander wide,
In sneakers bright, I try to glide,
Each step a dance, a wobbly spree,
As I chase my dreams, and trip on debris.

Avoiding puddles, my pants are a mess,
Laughing at mud, I couldn't care less,
In mismatched laces, I'm quite the sight,
Footloose and fancy, I skip through the night.

Footprints of the Heart

My flip-flops squeak like a rubber duck,
Every leap I take feels like pure luck,
With a skip and a hop, I dance through the park,
Leaving behind a trail, bright and stark.

In high-tops that sparkle, I strut and sway,
Making shadows do the cha-cha and play,
With each silly stomp, my worries fade,
As I tap-tap away, life's parade is made.

Soles Dancing on Asphalt

With every step, my soles go 'thud,'
Pavement beneath, and I'm covered in mud,
A twist and a turn, my balance is off,
My foot starts to slip, and then I just scoff.

But oh, what a sight! A dancer I be,
Wobbling wildly, so clumsily free,
In my funky kicks, I twirl and collide,
With laughter around me, I wade with pride.

The Journey in Every Step

With toes that tickle, I prance to the beat,
The ground sings beneath me with giggles so sweet,
Each stride a search for the best hidden snacks,
As my belly leads on, ignoring the cracks.

In clunky old boots, I stomp with delight,
Turning mundane walks into thrills of the night,
With every odd leap, my spirit runs free,
In life's silly dance, it's just you and me.

Soles that Seek

In a store, I found the perfect pair,
They squeak and squawk, but I don't care.
They'll lead me far, with style and flair,
But first, a dance—oh, beware the glare!

On cobblestones, they often trip,
As I attempt a fancy flip.
The locals laugh, I snag my zip,
But all in fun, a quirky quip!

With each step, adventure calls,
To laughter's tune, the mischief sprawls.
A puddle jump? Let's break the walls,
My laughter echoes, as good times thrall!

I find a trail, my spirits lift,
My trusty soles, a playful gift.
With every journey, the joys they sift,
Through rubbery puns, my worries drift!

Where the Footfalls Lead

On sidewalks cracked, where laughter thrives,
I wander 'round, where humor dives.
With each footfall, the city strives,
To keep me guessing where fun arrives.

Through puddles splashed, I'm feeling bold,
Tales of mishaps, easily told.
With every step, the humor's gold,
And on this path, my heart unfolds.

Lost in a maze of glittery shoes,
With neon lights, I spread my hues.
The world around, a myriad of views,
As laughter weaves, my spirit ensues!

The cobbles whisper tales of yore,
Each corner churns a brand-new score.
With silly socks, I dance on floor,
As giggles echo, forevermore!

Stitched in Wander

With stitching bright and colors bold,
I strut along, half-worn and old.
The stories trapped in every fold,
From tipsy trips, my heart's pure gold.

Each snag, a laugh, each rip, a jest,
In paths unknown, I'm feeling blessed.
With every step, a silly quest,
To find a treasure, oh, I'm compressed!

Through gardens lush and muddy fields,
My soles were magic, silver shields.
A stomp, a splash, the joy it yields,
In laughter's grip, my spirit wields!

Journeying on, where whims collide,
Through winding trails, I take my stride.
And in the chaos, I'll abide,
My stitched-up laugh, my gleeful guide!

Echoes of a Path Walked

On winding roads where giggles bloom,
I tread lightly, squish, and zoom.
With every echo, dispel the gloom,
As joy erupts, I'm in full bloom.

Old boots creak, but so does my laugh,
They stumble on, a playful gaffe.
Each turn reveals a crafty path,
In silly shoes, I feel the half!

Through fields of green, I leap with grace,
A dance routine, a funny chase.
With every step, a new embrace,
In whimsical stride, I find my place!

So let us wander, wild and free,
With laughter traced in every spree.
In this grand journey, it's clear to see,
The joy in steps, just you and me!

A Tapestry Woven in Footfalls

Each step a dance, we jig and twirl,
In boots so bright, watch colors swirl.
From heels to loafers, we stomp and glide,
Our merry march, a footwear ride.

With laces untied, and socks that clash,
We shuffle along, making quite a splash.
The world's our stage, with toes that sing,
In mismatched pairs, we're a goofy fling.

A tap of the toe, a wiggle of feet,
In a parade of gait, oh, isn't it sweet?
Our blunders are laughs, our stumbles bring cheer,
In this footloose fest, we've nothing to fear.

So lace up your laughter, and join the spree,
In a tapestry of steps, come jig with me!
No road too bumpy, no path too strange,
With soles of good humor, let's dance through change.

Muffin Tops and Moccasins

With muffin tops and comfy shoes,
We strut around with joyful views.
In this quirky town, we stomp and shuffle,
Each step a giggle, no hint of guffle.

Moccasins on, we glide with ease,
Like butter on toast, sailing through the breeze.
With every misstep, a chuckle arises,
Our feet like comedians, in fun disguises.

We march through puddles, splash and splatter,
In a world of chaos, our feet just flatter.
Our woes are few with each playful trot,
In muffin tops and moccasins, we've got the plot!

So join the jolly parade of the odd,
With laughter and footwear, let's give a nod.
In this whimsical waltz, our spirits will soar,
With muffin tops and moccasins, who could ask for more?

March of the Travelers

Pack up your giggles, it's time to roam,
With socks that clash, we've made it our home.
In this quirky trek, let's skip and cheer,
March of the travelers, let's shift up a gear!

With sandals squeaking and boots that clomp,
We swagger along, creating quite a stomp.
From city to summit, we paint the ground,
With every footfall, our joy is profound.

We trip over dreams, we dance with delight,
In this merry march, everything feels right.
Our footwear may wobble, our steps might stray,
But the laughter we share will light up the way.

So take off your worries, let silliness reign,
In the march of the travelers, we dance through the rain.
With each little stumble, we spread even cheer,
In this zany parade, we have nothing to fear!

Etched in Steps of Destiny

Every step we take, a story unfolds,
In shiny new kicks or ancient gold.
Wobbling along like a babbling brook,
In this grand adventure, let's take a look!

With flap and flounder, we dance through the day,
In funky fresh styles, we brightly sway.
With footpaths tangled, yet hearts so free,
Etched in our steps, we're all meant to be.

We giggle and grin, with laughter that swells,
Each misstep a tale that only time tells.
In the rhythm of life, we tap and prance,
In this dance of creation, let's take a chance!

So let's lace up laughter, embrace the absurd,
In every step taken, we'll spread the word.
Etched in our journey, our tales intertwine,
With footsteps of joy, our spirits align!

Sturdy Steps through Time

Worn-out soles and tales to tell,
Each scuff a memory, ringing like a bell.
From puddles splashed to stinky grass,
These trusty pals will help me pass.

With laces long and tongues that flop,
I trip and tumble, but still I hop.
The squeaks and creaks become my tune,
As I dance away beneath the moon.

Bumps and bruises add charm, oh dear!
My buddies grumble but I simply cheer.
With every step, I giggle and glide,
In this wild adventure, they're my pride.

So here's to kicks that have seen it all,
Worn with joy, they still stand tall.
Through mud and grit, our bond is tight,
Together we conquer, morning to night.

Awakened from the Ground Up

From closet depths, they beg to roam,
Two perilous pals, never far from home.
I lace them up, we're ready to leave,
With a hop, skip, jump, oh what a weave!

They whisper jokes while I trot along,
In every crevice, they hum a song.
Suddenly shiny, they twirl with glee,
As I dodge the hurdles that life throws at me.

With goofy prints and colors so bright,
They make a statement, what a sight!
Through ups and downs, on paths of fun,
These clumsy friends shine like the sun.

So off we go, through thick and thin,
In this dance of steps, we start to spin.
With every march, we cause a stir,
Two adventurers ready to mutter and purr.

Quest of the Well-Traveled

On this epic trek, they're my faithful allies,
Cracks and crevices, oh, what a surprise!
Packed with stories, both silly and bright,
Every scuff a chapter in our shared plight.

From the sidewalk run to the beach-time play,
They chase away troubles, come what may.
With shoelaces tangled in a ridiculous mess,
We laugh at each slip, oh, what a stress!

Along rocky trails, we gallop and bounce,
A hilarious trio that is sure to pounce.
My companions grumble, but I can't complain,
For every misstep becomes a refrain.

So here's to the journey, with paths yet to chart,
In this voyage of laughter, they play a part.
Forever we wander, together in rhyme,
As we dance through the echoes of whimsical time.

The Canvas of Our Path

With every step, new colors emerge,
Painting our journey where laughter can surge.
The soles of my life, they gather the dust,
A splash of adventure, oh how I trust!

Each printed pattern, a story to share,
A canvas of journeys, woven with care.
From gum stuck tight to graffiti bright,
They sprinkle our tales with sheer delight.

Sidewalks become our canvas, bold and grand,
As we skip through the chaos, hand in hand.
With a wiggle, dance, and a chuckle carefree,
Life's little mishaps bring joy to me.

So let's step forward, paint our own way,
With whimsy and laughter, come what may.
For every twist and turn, we'll shout and we'll cheer,
With hearts full of joy and nothing to fear.

The Road Beneath My Feet

I've got a pair, not quite the same,
One squeaks loud, the other's to blame.
They dance on cobbles, they slide in rain,
With feet like mine, it's hard to complain.

The asphalt whispers, secrets it keeps,
While my left foot chuckles, the right one sleeps.
In mismatched fashion, I swagger with flair,
My toes peek out; I toss back my hair.

Each creak and clatter, a comedic tune,
While dodging puddles like a cartoon.
With every step, fun moments bloom,
Ahead lies laughter, behind is the gloom.

So here I go, on this wobbly path,
With shoes that giggle, I'll take on the math.
Each toe's a buddy, we laugh and we trot,
Together we stumble; it's quite a lot!

Laces Untied in Adventure

Oh, the laces flapping, in the wind they fly,
Like wild birds cackling in a blue sky.
One's a lefty, the other a right,
In this tug-of-war, I'm losing the fight.

Tripping with laughter, I tumble and roll,
Chasing a dream like a wayward shoal.
The knots come undone, but who really cares?
I trip over joy, as the world shares my flares.

Each step is a dance; a new comic act,
With every misstep, I'm plotting my pact.
These laces, they lead to adventures galore,
Untied and wild, who could ask for more?

So let them unbuckle, let mischief take flight,
With my untamed treads, I'll jive through the night.
Each bounce keeps me young, don't catch me in strife,
With laces untied, I'm dancing with life!

Every Step Tells a Story

With each little hop, there's a tale to tell,
Of sidewalks and pavements, I know them well.
Each scuff and scratch holds a secret or two,
In this goofy saga, I stumble for you.

A pigeon's my witness; he shakes his head,
As I flounder and fumble, just want to get fed.
The stories I gather from taps and from treads,
Bring giggles and chuckles; I'll dance till I'm dead.

The squares I step in are paved with delight,
In every misstep, there's a giggle, a bite.
I leap through the puddles, splash high as I can,
Each hop is a chapter, and here comes the plan.

So laugh with me now, let's take this long way,
With shoes that are silly, we'll brighten the day.
In every adventure, together we'll trot,
For every step taken is a story, a plot!

The Color of My Path

On a path painted brightly, I skip and I hop,
With feet like a rainbow, I'll never stop.
My sandals gleam yellow, my sneakers are blue,
Each step's a giggle; who knew this was true?

Through puddles of color, I dance with a grin,
My feet are the artists, let the fun begin.
With splashes of laughter, my canvas is wide,
Painting the world as I splatter and glide.

Each hue tells a story, in rhythm and rhyme,
With each dazzling moment, I'm lost in the clime.
The landscapes are giggling, the skies start to play,
With colors of joy, I'll paint my own way.

So join in the fun, let's color outside,
With every small journey, let humor be our guide.
Step after step, let the world be our art,
Every vibrant footfall's a laugh from the heart!

The Essence of Exploration

With laces that long like corndog sticks,
I wander the world with my clumsy kicks.
Each step a dance, a laugh, a sway,
Who knew the ground could have such play?

I stomp through puddles, make splashes galore,
Like a kid again, I can't help but explore.
These funny things on my feet, divine,
They trip me up, but oh, they're mine!

My soles may be frail, but my spirit is bold,
With stories of mischief just waiting to be told.
Each toe a captain, so gallant, so grand,
Leading the charge through this glorious land.

And when I return, they'll sit by the door,
Tired and worn, but oh, what a score!
For every misstep and stumblin' chat,
I'll treasure these moments, how silly is that?

Treading on Horizons

I bought a pair that squeak and beep,
They're such a joy, I can't help but leap.
Across the grass, I give a great hop,
My feet are a band, and I'm their top bop!

With each bold step, they wiggle and smile,
Creating a ruckus every single mile.
These comic co-stars in my grand parade,
Enjoy the laughter, the fun they made.

I chase my dreams and sometimes I slip,
A little tip here, a wobbly trip.
But they just laugh—a jolly old crew,
On this amusing path, there's nothing I rue.

So here's to the soles that carry my weight,
With their goofy antics, they've sealed my fate.
Though they might be odd, in color, in tone,
They plod through life, never alone!

Embodied Paths and Rhythms

Oh, the blisters tell tales of places I've gone,
These characters worn, they have never withdrawn.
They've danced through the rain and wobbled through
glee,
A riot of laughter, just wait and see!

In my mismatched pair, I strut like a star,
Each step is a giggle, no matter how far.
With each little stomp, I compose a new beat,
A rhythm of joy, can't be beat with defeat!

Looking for pirates or chasing the breeze,
My feet are explorers, they do as they please.
And when I trip over my own silly lace,
I just burst out laughing, embrace the wild space!

So here's to the heroes that carry my dreams,
With each quirky step, life's richer, it seems.
More than mere items, they dance and they sing,
Oh, the delight that each journey can bring!

The Unseen Trail

Where do we wander, on paths unseen?
With these quirky companions, my journey's routine.
They skip and they shuffle, with flair and with style,
Making mundane trips feel joyous and worthwhile.

I treat every step like a wacky parade,
As goofy as cartoons, a mix-up charade.
With each little hop, there's a giggle or two,
Exploring the world in this nutty shoe crew!

I've left footprints of laughter down every lane,
Silly moments abound, no reason for pain.
These trusty sidekicks, they jive and they rock,
Creating a symphony on every block.

So let's wander onward, with zest on the trail,
With joy as our compass, we'll never go pale.
In steps of hilarity, we'll conquer the day,
In the dance of this journey, let laughter hold sway!

The Path Left Behind

Laces flown like a kite in the breeze,
Treading lightly, we dance with ease.
Each step a giggle, a hop, a skip,
Tripping over dreams—oh, what a trip!

Dust and mud, a quirky attire,
Finding puddles, oh what a mire!
Avoid that wet sock, it squeaks like a mouse,
Who knew adventure lived in this house?

From cobblestones to grassy fields,
Where tangled terrain the laughter yields.
With every stumble, a funny glance,
Life's a clumsy and carefree dance!

Hold on tight, our path's a jest,
As we march on, we're truly blessed.
With each new twist and silly turn,
We'll laugh it off and always learn!

Beneath My Arc of Journey

Underneath arches of old, creaky wood,
I shuffle and shuffle, oh, this feels good!
With each strange noise, my feet start to squeak,
Is that a shoe or a hungry beak?

Colors so bright, a carnival flare,
My soles do the tango, without a care.
With every misstep and comic flare,
I'm king of the world, just look at my hair!

Around the corners where shadows do creep,
My soles have a secret, but it's hard to keep.
They whisper of trips and mischief galore,
What wonders await? Let's explore some more!

Through laughter and folly, my path starts to bend,
In this grand circus, there's fun without end.
With each tiny wobble, I face life anew,
Oh, what a journey beneath skies so blue!

Unraveled Laces of Adventure

Tangled laces, they dance in the air,
With a twirl and a twist, oh, what a pair!
They trip up my feet like playful kittens,
Turning my strides into giggly smittens!

A runaway sock takes off with a bang,
Giggling bubbles in each little clang.
With every jog, there's a giddy shout,
Who knew adventure was so knocked about?

In fields of green, my laces unwind,
Sprinting for freedom; oh, how they're blind.
But laughter breaks out, we're having a blast,
Who knew the fun could race by so fast?

With every fall, another wacky tale,
From sweat and grins, we'll never frail.
For tangled laces keep us in play,
In this wild run, we're living our way!

The Unsung Steps

Steps that bobble, steps that sway,
Like a dance party on a busy highway.
Each footfall echoes like a clown's big shoe,
Tiptoeing into mischief, it's what we do!

The laughter spills forth, a fountain of cheer,
As each little moment brings a grin near.
With funny little jiggles, we stomp and clap,
In this lively parade, there's always a gap!

To strut down the lane, a whimsical roam,
Every turn an invitation—let's bring it home!
We'll shake off the dust and dance in delight,
When the world is a stage, the future's so bright!

So here's to the steps that take us afar,
To the rhythm of life, each silliness a star.
In this merry-go-round of flops and flips,
We're the unsung heroes in our own little quips!

Terrain of the Traveler

Beneath my feet, a carpet wide,
With bumps and dips, my trusty guide.
A flip-flop here, a sneaker there,
Each step I take, I feel the flare.

The pavement laughs, the gravel grins,
As I do dance, while fate begins.
A puddle splashes, oh what a kick,
Mud on my toes? Well, that's my trick!

Adventure calls from every crack,
With each misstep, I don't look back.
Through fields of grass, I chase a deer,
While tripping over, "Oops! Not here!"

So on I hop, in silly stride,
Laughing at all, with joy inside.
Each rocky patch, a chance to grin,
These quirky lands, my road of sin!

The Heartbeat of the Pathway.

In every stomp, a rhythm loud,
The dirt responds, oh I'm so proud!
With each quick step, my soles do sing,
To all the perks that travel brings.

A fancy lace, a knot so tight,
Yet still I trip, what a delight!
I leap like frogs and shuffle slow,
The journey's dance, a quirky show.

Worn-out tread, a badge of cheer,
Each crack a story from yesteryear.
With every shuffle, a little jig,
I find my stride, it's getting big!

A hop, a skip, a slide, oh me!
These winding roads are wild and free.
So join the fun, let's take a stroll,
Together we'll fix each little hole!

Paths Beneath My Soles

On bustling streets, my soles do glide,
A comedy show, when I decide.
For every block, a tale to share,
With wobbly moves and wild flair.

Tap-dancing down, I sway and swerve,
A sidewalk stage, I have the nerve.
With every step, a story spins,
Oh, how the world enjoys my sins!

Through puddles deep, I take a leap,
Splashing onlookers, it's mine to keep.
A trail of laughter, a squishy mess,
Among the fun, I feel so blessed!

So skip along, with joy untamed,
In every footfall, I'm unashamed.
The paths reflect each giggle and jest,
With every clumsy dance, I'm truly blessed!

Footprints of Dreams

With every step, my dreams extend,
Across the grass, where giggles blend.
A shuffle here, a twirl over there,
Each footprint whispers, "Dare to care!"

Mismatched socks dance side by side,
On pebble paths, they glide and slide.
A clumsy trip, a skip, a bound,
In silly antics, joy is found!

Through sticky streets, I leave my mark,
Like stories shared, igniting sparks.
The world's a stage, where laughter gleams,
In every step, I chase my dreams!

So strut your stuff, in zany glee,
With every move, be wild and free.
For life's a journey, filled with fun,
Let's dance together 'til we're done!

Worn Soles and Winding Roads

My sneakers sigh with every step,
The soles are thin, the threads are kept.
They grip the ground, but dance with grace,
On wobbly paths, we quicken pace.

Each puddle splashed, a tiny jest,
My flip-flops laugh, they like the fest.
They squeak and squish, a comic tune,
As if to say, 'Let's leave, and soon!'

Old boots complain, they creak and moan,
While sneakers shine like they're on loan.
A hefty laugh from sandals wide,
"Don't trip on air, just enjoy the ride!"

So, here we stomp, a jolly band,
On cracked old pavement, across the sand.
With soles that trip, we share our cheer,
For every step, there's fun, my dear!

Paths Beneath Our Feet

I chose a path with lots of pebbles,
My shoes now sound like tiny rebels.
They crackle like popcorn—what a noise!
My friends all laugh, and it brings joys.

One boot's too tight and feels like doom,
The other one wants to dance and zoom.
A squishy slip or toast to fate,
Each funky step is worth the wait!

With muddy patches all around,
A slip and slide, oh what a sound!
We wade through goo, our spirits high,
Dirty toes, yet we still fly!

Paths beneath us seem so grand,
When worn with humor, side-by-hand.
From concrete jungles to nature's bliss,
Each shoe a tale, none would we miss!

The Lace of Life

A tangle here, a knot undone,
My laces drag, but oh, what fun!
They trip me up, they pull and tease,
As if to say, 'Hey, run with ease!'

I tie them tight, they laugh in glee,
To trip and laugh is key, you see.
With every clash, they twist and twirl,
A ribbon circus for the world!

I'll hop and skip through sidewalks bright,
With loosely tied smiles, pure delight.
Oh life's a game, with laces long,
We stumble through our silly song!

Let's loosen up, let's set them free,
For life's a dance with laughter's spree.
When laces play, we'll twirl around,
In this wild waltz, pure joy is found!

Treads of Tomorrow

My treads are worn, but oh so proud,
They lead me boldly, shout out loud.
With slicks and slides, and marks divine,
A comical journey, all mine to twine!

Each scuff tells tales of where I've been,
From muddy trails to streets so clean.
With every step, a silly slip,
And giggles echo, how we flip!

Tomorrow beckons with shoes so bright,
Worn soles dance beneath the light.
With every twist and every turn,
There's laughter waiting, lessons learned.

So let's embrace each quirky tread,
For every giggle, no need for dread.
In the journey ahead, we'll bound and leap,
With funny steps and memories we keep!

Lacing Up Life's Journey

I put on my best sneakers, ready to run,
With laces that tangle like jokes, oh what fun!
Each step's a surprise, a small twisty route,
I skip over puddles while dancing about.

Flip-flops in winter? That can't be right!
My toes are all chilly, oh what a sight!
But each little misstep is part of the game,
Life's goofy parade, we're all just the same.

In socks with bold stripes, I sprint to the door,
But trip on my cat—now that's quite the score!
She looks at me slyly, I call it a tie,
Together we tumble, oh me, oh my!

From flip-flops to crocs, I measure my day,
Each shoe tells a story, come laugh if you may.
In mismatched old boots, let's waltz with a cheer,
Life's quirky footwear is all we hold dear.

Footprints in Time

Tiny shoes left at the door,
Each one a story, who could ask for more?
A line of mismatched pairs, what a view,
The house feels alive, with much to pursue.

Slippers and sandals, all tossed in a heap,
Each pause in the hallway, a laugh to keep.
I step on a rubber duck, hear it squeak,
As I journey and tumble, it's fun, not bleak.

At the beach, we leave prints, oh, what a show,
A parade of our antics, dancing just so.
But the tide sweeps them away with a grin,
Life's like that, we laugh, then we begin.

So cherish each footprint, both silly and small,
In moonlight or sunlight, embrace through it all.
With quirky little shoes, let's skip and let gleam,
What's left behind is a giggle supreme.

Wear and Tear of Adventures

Old boots with good stories, they've traveled afar,
Each scuff holds a memory, a laughter-filled scar.
Laces just frayed, but they hold strong the tales,
Of hiking up hills and navigating gales.

In rainbow bright sneakers, I bounce and I trip,
They squeak as I skip, what a comical slip!
One eye on the road, the other on snacks,
Life's just as fun with those glorious cracks.

Worn-out flats parked by the fire,
Gathering dust, but oh, they inspire!
A dance through the air, hoot and a holler,
My toes keep on wiggling, the neighbors now scarier.

Curled-up sandals, out for the season,
Each story is silly, and there's always a reason.
Through wear and through tear, they're part of my art,
These crazy companions, they've stolen my heart.

A Dance of Soles

With jiggly little toes, I start off the beat,
My shoes are like dancers, all ready to meet!
Flamenco in flats, a cha-cha in boots,
When socks join the fun, it's a party, for shoots!

Oh chaos ensues with each twirl and spin,
A slide on the kitchen floor, laughter begins.
One shoe goes left while the other goes right,
A dance-off of madness that lasts through the night.

In sandals that squeak, we sway to the sound,
As balloons in our hands go bopping around.
Each misstep's a giggle, a tap on the floor,
Life's rhythm is silly, let's dance some more!

From clogs to bright trainers, let soles take flight,
In a jig of delight, we'll shine through the night.
With movements so quirky, our hearts will collide,
In this merry ballet, let's always abide!

Echoes Beneath the Arch

Beneath the arch where echoes play,
My soles slip-slide, come what may.
With each loud squawk, a pigeon flies,
Chasing my dreams, it's no surprise.

My left shoe squeaks like a sad old duck,
The right one dances, oh what luck!
Together they create a merry tune,
While I just hope I don't trip on a broom.

Sidewalks become my endless stage,
Where every step is a new page.
A tap, a twirl, my feet take flight,
But gravity says, "Not tonight!"

I slip on gum like a daring feat,
With every wobble, I skip a beat.
Yet laughter follows, it never ends,
In shoes that make me trip with friends.

Odysseys in Old Leather

In leather worn that tells a tale,
I stomp my feet, I jig, I sail.
Each scuff a badge, each crease a mark,
My journey bold, igniting spark.

The lace unties, I take a chance,
To tango with my clumsy dance.
Oh look! A squirrel, it darts and swerves,
I trip again; my fate preserves!

"Hey, catch me if you can!" they yell,
But I'm busy dodging every shell.
With ponderous steps, I brave the street,
My leather shoes, they just can't beat!

Old sandals whisper with a grin,
Contemplating troubles where I've been.
Adventure waits in every scuff,
And I just laugh, this life's enough!

The Comfort of New Horizons

I bought new kicks that squeak with joy,
Like a rambunctious, playful toy.
They bounce and jive, what a fine show,
Each leap I make, I steal the glow.

Staring at clouds that wear a fluff,
I wiggle my toes, just silly stuff.
These snazzy friends are bold, not meek,
They love to strut and hear me speak!

But muddy puddles—what's that about?
A hop, a splash, I scream and shout!
"I'm a mermaid!" I proclaim with glee,
While the world just laughs and starts to flee.

With every step, a new surprise,
These sneakers show me endless skies.
"Oops, I didn't mean to tread on you!"
One stumble leads to "Love you too!"

Unraveled Threads of Adventure

With threads unraveling, oh dear me,
My sandals shout, "Come play, let's be!"
Each tiny string a rumor loud,
As I parade before the crowd.

I tripped on dreams on a sunny morn,
My laces tied in bows went torn.
Yet every fall, a giggle shared,
With buskers clapping, they cared!

Beneath the sun, I'll walk the line,
With mismatched flair, it's simply fine.
With every step, my heart will race,
What's life without a silly face?

From sidewalk art to puddled rain,
Every journey, a fun refrain.
So here I dance, a silly thread,
With laughter trailing where I tread.

Through Dust and Dreams

In dusty trails where socks do roam,
My sandals squeak, they call me home.
With every step, the stories bloom,
But oh, these blisters bring such gloom.

I slip and slide on path so steep,
Each tumble brings a laugh, not a weep.
My laces untie like they conspire,
To trip me up, I'm such a flyer.

A twist, a turn, a snag on grass,
I wonder if this journey's a pass.
With laughter ringing, I seize each stride,
While dust clouds form, they are my guide.

So here I go, with mismatched flair,
I dance with rhythm, without a care.
The paths are wild, my heart's a beam,
Through every laugh, I stitch my dream.

Treading on Tomorrow

Tomorrow's roads, a mystery wide,
With colorful kicks and open stride.
Each step I take is a surprised fling,
Like hopping on one foot, what will it bring?

My sneakers squeal with joy and fright,
They tell me tales all through the night.
A leap of faith, a hopscotch ground,
The quirk of fate, so often found.

Dodging puddles, my socks get soaked,
Yet every slip brings a giggle stoked.
But cautious wandering leads to a dance,
So bring on the laughter, it's worth a chance!

On tomorrow's path, I strut with flair,
Unbothered, carefree, without a care.
With playful feet, I trot along,
In jumbled rhythms, I find my song.

The Leather of Adventure

Adventure calls with leather creaks,
I stumble forth, and laughter leaks.
With every trip, my stride's a mess,
Yet here I go, no time to stress.

These rugged soles tell tales so bold,
Of paths untaken and treasures untold.
But who knew that mud could fly so high?
Just now I'm a cake, and that's no lie!

Each scuffed toe reveals a tale,
Of coffee spills and laughing trails.
With hops and skips, I chase the sun,
Who needs finesse? Here, it's all just fun!

Through tangled reeds, I prance and roam,
In every stumble, I find my home.
So raise a cheer for my beleaguered soles,
For leather dreams and adventurous goals.

Starlit Paths and Scuffed Souls

Under starlit skies, my soles shine bright,
With scars and stories, they take flight.
Each step's a dance in a goofy way,
Who knew the moon would join my play?

I trip on rocks and laugh in delight,
These scuffed old friends keep me upright.
In nighttime journeys, shadows can tease,
But nothing's better than a midnight breeze!

With every twist, oh what a laugh,
I do the tango, a clumsy half.
In the glow of laughter, I find my grace,
Embracing the joy of this wild space.

So here I wander beneath the stars,
With scuffed old soles, I'm a dance with scars.
Adventure awaits, let's frolic and cheer,
Every clumsy step holds memories dear.

Trails of Memory and Mud

In puddles deep, I took a leap,
My boots now squish, and socks do weep.
Each step a splash, a giggle loud,
With muddy prints, I'm quite proud.

The path is slick, I dance and trip,
Like a cartoon, I start to slip.
But laughter echoes through the trees,
As nature chuckles with the breeze.

A worm waves up, a greeting bright,
"Hey you there! What a silly sight!"
I tip my hat, my heart a flutter,
In this wild mess of muck and clutter.

At journey's end, I stand and pose,
My muddy feet, like art, they glow.
In every trace, a tale to tell,
Of joyful slips, I know so well.

The Journey Within My Soles

Each morning starts with a squishy feel,
A sock tucked under, a strange appeal.
My sandals squeak like they have a voice,
In quirky chorus, they rejoice!

I stroll past folks with fancy strides,
While I parade in my what-the-heck glides.
They raise an eyebrow, I give a grin,
In my wobbly kicks, I'm bound to win!

When left foot trips on a hidden clue,
Right foot says, "Dude, what's wrong with you?"
We argue loud, like an old couple,
But together we conquer every puddle.

So here I dance with a silly flair,
In colorful patterns, I'm beyond compare.
My soles carry tales, both big and small,
In this happy march, I'll never stall.

Where Canvas Meets Concrete

My sneakers squeak on urban streets,
A ruckus made with every beat.
The canvas bright — oh what a sight,
As I strut past pedestrians, feeling light.

The pigeons scatter, pecking in fright,
"When did this joker call us a flight?"
I laugh and whirl, a dizzy twirl,
In this grand escapade, my heart will pearl.

With splashes of color like candy spritz,
Each step's a hop and a little blitz.
I dodge the cracks, a game of skill,
Concrete jungle, I'll bend to your thrill.

And when the sunset paints the town,
In windy heaves, I lose my frown.
Feet tapping softly like secret spies,
In my vibrant kicks, I touch the skies.

Beyond the Worn Out

These soles are cracked, the laces frayed,
They've seen some things, I'm not afraid.
From dashing home to muddy trails,
My trusty kicks tell grand details.

Every scuff a memory, every tear a grin,
I stumble and tumble, yet always win.
With laughter laced through every stride,
Together we tackle the wild outside.

Through grass and gravel, we leap and bound,
In this rugged life, till laughter's found.
I trip and roll, the grass my bed,
With a wink in my shoe, I forge ahead.

So here's to the soles with tales to share,
Each worn-out tread a badge of flair.
With funny steps, I embrace the grind,
In the circus of life, I'm one of a kind.

Trails of the Heart

In a closet, they peek with glee,
Waiting for adventures, just like me.
One's too tight, another's too loose,
Yet all promise fun, a merry truce.

They've danced in puddles and splashed in mud,
Forging new paths where the wild things thud.
With squeaks and creaks, they sing their tune,
Two left feet hoping they'll learn to swoon.

Each pair tells tales of places we roam,
From sidewalks to trails that feel like home.
Though bruised and battered, they wear it proud,
Dirty and loud, they shout out loud!

So lace them tight, let's take a chance,
Join the parade; come on, let's dance!
With laughter echoing, we'll twirl and spin,
In every mishap, together we win!

The Weight of My Steps

With every stride, my soles complain,
'Why oh why do you love this pain?'
Each step a story, heavy and light,
Paving my path from morning to night.

Worn-out canvas, what a sight to see,
Hiding secrets they've shared with me.
Got creaky arches and swaggering flair,
Like they're about to break into a dare.

In the shoes of my mischief, I stomp and prance,
Each misstep's a reason to giggle and dance.
They squeak with delight at every mistake,
Whispering 'take risks!' for laughter's sake.

So hold your breath when I take a leap,
These soles are heroes, they're never cheap!
Through puddles and mud, they drag and slide,
Together we tackle this joyful ride!

Journey's Rhythm

My sneakers shuffle, a tap and a tap,
Trying to dance but caught in a flap.
They squeak like a squeaky toy in delight,
Join in the rhythm, let's groove through the night.

With every step, they drum on the ground,
A slapstick performance, check out the sound!
From sunny beaches to treacherous hills,
They huff and puff while I seek the thrills.

Socked and sandaled, oh what a sight,
Hiding in bushes from a surprise fright.
In mismatched colors, they tell a tale,
Of whimsical trips through the wind and hail.

They twist and turn, toe-tapping with glee,
Through ditches and sidewalks, what fun to see!
With every faff and every stumble,
They echo in laughter, making hearts tumble!

In the Shadow of My Treads

In quiet corners, they quietly sigh,
'Why must you put us through all this try?'
As I bounce through the day, they plot with flair,
Joining in fun with odd styles to wear.

Each scuff and scrape tells a tale of sass,
From backyard picnics to skipping class.
They whisper sweet nothings to mud and grass,
Creating a canvas, a charming morass.

Sometimes they trip, in a comedy flight,
A fountain of laughter exploding in sight.
With every misstep, they giggle and cheer,
'Let's make a memory, don't shed a tear!'

So here we march, in rhythm we tread,
With memory's burden, but laughter instead.
The journey is wild, with stories galore,
Together we wander, forever encore!

Whispers in Every Step

Each step I take, oh what a sound,
My sneakers squeak, they're quite renowned.
They chat and giggle as I walk along,
In this quirky dance, I feel so strong.

With every stomp, a tale they weave,
Of silly moments, I can't believe.
They slip and slide, they jump and sway,
Oh, what a show, come join the play!

I tried some boots, they were too tight,
They grumbled low, not feeling right.
But flip-flops sing their breezy tune,
While I bounce around like a cartoon!

Each stride a story, each pause a jest,
With all my footwear, I am truly blessed.
So here I prance on this merry spree,
In the wacky world of walk with glee!

The Trail of Life

Life's a path, with gravel and muck,
My sandals squeak, what the … oh, stuck!
They chuckle back, like cheeky friends,
Supporting me through twists and bends.

A moccasin mocks as I step on a stone,
'Better than blisters,' it makes a groan.
I leap through puddles, dance in the rain,
My footwear gripes, but they love the game.

I tried to sprint with leather so fine,
But tripped on laces, oh what a sign!
Now I strut in crocs, with flair and ease,
They flip and flop, like a gentle breeze.

Each moment a laugh, each trip a cheer,
With soles that grip tight, what do I fear?
Adventure awaits, in every stride,
Let's skip along with joy and pride!

Traveling in Solitude

In quiet moments, my shoes softly sigh,
'Here we go again,' as I wave good-bye.
With every step, they take the lead,
An awkward dance, oh, such a speed!

They tiptoe softly through the woods,
Where ants hold shows, in little hoods.
A rogue pebble jumps right in my way,
My footwear laughs, 'It's just our play!'

I wander alone, but not really so,
Each tap and clack is a friendly hello.
My clogs make clamor, it's hard to be shy,
As I strut through life, giving a pie-in-the-sky.

Though solitude whispers, I'm never alone,
With each playful step, I've built my throne.
In the dance of the soles, I find my way,
With giggles and quirks, I seize the day!

The Soles of the Storyteller

In worn-out shoes that tell my tale,
Each scuff a chapter, my feet set sail.
The tales they share, of mishaps and cheer,
With every shuffle, I hold them dear.

I've stumbled on paths both muddy and bright,
Tripped over tales late in the night.
With each cursed rock, my shoes break free,
Whispering secrets, just for me.

My slippers giggle when I hit the floor,
'Another adventure,' they seem to implore.
Each typo stomp when I tell a yarn,
Turns tales to legends, like a boastful charm.

With soles so rich, full of bliss,
They've walked through storms, and that's no miss!
So listen closely when I stride on through,
My footwear have stories, just like you!

Footsteps in the Dust

With each step, the sand does fly,
I'm a walking cloud, oh my oh my!
Every footprint, a giggle, a laugh,
Trying to dance on this sandy path.

The crabs must think I'm quite the sight,
Doing the cha-cha in morning light.
My toes are tickled, my ankles spray,
In the wiggly wiggle of the sandy play.

But when I stop, the dust will cling,
To my legs like I'm wearing a spring.
I'll shake it off, but a friend bursts out,
"Do you know you're a dust bunny about?"

A lesson learned, I now declare:
Dance your way without a care!
So I prance and hop, and guess what's true—
Dust will follow, it's part of the crew!

The Weight We Carry

My backpack's heavy, like a brick,
With snacks and books that do the trick.
Each step I take, I feel the strain,
But I'm off to see the sky again!

I load it up with things galore,
Mismatched socks and a rubber dinosaur.
Why do I carry this mountain of stuff?
Because who knows when I'll need a plush puff?

Along the path, I start to sway,
My balance wobbles, oh not today!
With every tumble, I learn for sure:
Less is more, but what's life without a tour?

So let's pack light and skip with glee,
Adventure awaits, just you and me!
We'll ditch the burden and dance away,
With laughter and smiles upon our play!

Journeys in Every Size

Big boots stomp, oh what a sound!
Tiny toes tap, barely on ground.
A mismatched pair walks side by side,
With a giggle, they take it in stride.

Flippers flopping, with much delight,
Heads turning as they take flight.
One in heels, the other in slides,
Together they conquer the world's wild rides.

"Size doesn't matter," they refine,
"We'll bounce around, feeling fine!
From puddles to puddles, we'll take the chance,
In every odd shoe, we'll find our dance!"

And off they go, hand in hand,
A stroll through chaos, oh so grand.
In every size, there's fun to share,
As long as laughter finds us everywhere!

Souls in Soles

There's magic in the soles we wear,
Each scrape a mark, a tale to share.
In flip-flops squeak and boots that shine,
Every journey a stitch in time.

My sandals laugh, they're quite the pair,
With stories spun from summer air.
One lost a cousin in the park,
Now it hops about, lit by spark!

Ode to the sneakers with shoelaces long,
They sprint through life, they've got the song.
With every mile, they start to tire,
But still, they dance, like they're on fire!

"We're all a crew," the soles proclaim,
"From high heel royalty to the running game.
Let's stomp and clap, our duty is clear,
Life's a riot with good friends near!

Steps Etched in Memory

On paths where laughter lit the way,
My toes poked through in bright array.
Each scuff and scrape a tale to tell,
Of clumsy stumbles and lasting fell.

Green grass stains on a sunny day,
Hiccups in stride like a dance ballet.
With every slip a giggle's spring,
Life's a party, and I'm the king!

Bouncing off puddles, a joyous splash,
Who knew mud could be such a bash?
Squeaky sounds in a serious crowd,
Echoes of laughter, oh so loud!

Now peeking in at that dusty pair,
They still hold memories beyond compare.
Each scuffed and faded, perfect as ever,
In the wardrobe of my life, a funny endeavor!

Wanders into the Unknown

With every step, I take a chance,
On grass so tall, I start to dance.
Lost in thought, I trip on air,
A tumble down in a wild affair.

One foot in puddles, the other in grass,
I wave to the squirrels as they pass.
A leap of faith into a mud pie,
Those pesky birds mock with a fly.

The world's a runway where I am bold,
In sneakers bright, my stories unfold.
A twist, a turn, a backwards glide,
In every stumble, there's joy to bide.

Through fields of daisies, I take a flop,
Turning my mishaps into a hop.
So here I go, the unknown awaits,
With a heart so light, let's tempt the fates!

The Ground We Cover

Oh, the paths we pave in giggles and cheer,
From tiptoes to leaps, not a shadow of fear.
Each stride a burst of mischief and fun,
Every scuffle a dance, we've only begun.

Chasing after clouds, racing the sun,
What's life without gaffes? It's never a run!
Over a stump or a squirrel or two,
With bumps and giggles, out of the blue!

Asphalt or gravel, it's all just a game,
Let's walk on the wild side, it's never the same.
A twirl, a spin, in the moonlight's daze,
Each step like a song, in a quirky phase.

Our footprints etched in a comical cast,
In places we wander, fun shadows are cast.
So gather your spirit, let's dance and play,
With laughter in our hearts, come what may!

Memories Worn in Tread

A pair of spacers, with colors ablaze,
Worn down by laughter, in playful displays.
Chasing down dreams, they bounce and they flip,
A gliding sensation with each little trip.

They've jumped through puddles, they've walked on air,
Each nick tells a story, a wild affair.
Grass stains and crumbs of snacks along the way,
In this joyful ride, let's make it a play!

With soles that squeal and laces untied,
Who needs grace when you've got such pride?
We dance past the sunset, arm in arm,
In a tumble of giggles, there's always charm!

So here's to the moments, both silly and dear,
In the journey of life, let's cast away fear.
Let's wear out these memories, together in glee,
For every takeoff writes our own wild decree!